Beauties of the octagonal pool

Beauties of the octagonal pool
Gregory O'Brien

AUCKLAND UNIVERSITY PRESS

for Jenny, Jack-Marcel, Felix and Carlo

First published 2012

Auckland University Press
University of Auckland
Private Bag 92019
Auckland 1142, New Zealand
www.press.auckland.ac.nz

Poems and drawings © Gregory O'Brien, 2012

ISBN 978 1 86940 579 3

Publication is kindly assisted by &creative*nz*
ARTS COUNCIL OF NEW ZEALAND TOI AOTEAROA

National Library of New Zealand Cataloguing-in-Publication Data
O'Brien, Gregory, 1961-
Beauties of the octagonal pool / Gregory O'Brien.
ISBN 978-1-86940-579-3
I. Title.
NZ821.2—dc 22

Front cover image: Gregory O'Brien, *In anticipation of seamounts,
flying fish* (2011), acrylic on canvas, 610 x 475mm

Cover design: Kalee Jackson

Printed by 1010 Printing International Ltd

Contents

4. Red square, black square

5. Little Oneroa

6. Among trees

7. *Romantic voyage*

8. *The invisible fathers*

Rubens, desirous of expressing the calm
and serenity of his existence,
paints himself in company

with his wife in his garden,
in the midst of an ascent
of vertical lines.

But when he has to paint battles
or storms he submits
the whole composition

to a system of spirals, the unfolding
of which over the surface
and in depth

can be reduced to the diagram
of acanthus leaves and tendrils
reproduced above.

      —from André Lhote,
      Treatise on Landscape Painting

1. Beauties of the octagonal pool

The lake of first girlfriends

There was nothing to swim for
but swimming itself
          a bright patch

a faintly distracted air
about her. And a safe distance
          from shore

ramps upon which
the water-skiers among us
          were sporadically lifted

above themselves and from where
they could survey a shoreline
          of discarded shoes

a ball-gown to drown
in. There was nothing to swim for
          but a respite

from swimming. A millpond.
A parting of her hair
          wake of a speedboat

a moment past.

Whangaparoa, 1975

It was a time more than
a place, this side

of the grass court. And those youngest
of opponents

forever advancing towards us—a Rachel,
a Catherine, a Jenny,

another Rachel—they came so close
it was as if they really

existed. The boys, for the most part, were
a few years behind

but catching up. We toiled and troubled,
we swam home

after the dance. There were indentations in our bodies
from sleeping on couch grass

or next to unfamiliar objects—a magnet,
a stray bone or broken

necklace. Someone read a book, another became
a priest. We all went

overboard. Someone put that book
down. It was love.

By late afternoon the grass courts
that had once

been so inviting seemed distracted, oblivious
to us. And the lawns, without which

youth would never have been complete, it was
a breeze from far beyond us

that groomed and ruffled, that
completed them.

Pencil

Even if yachts were moored
mid-air, the clouds ill-rendered
and the birds far from
aerodynamic, somehow

he got you right—in the
dwindling light, with its
rugs, shawls, chimneys,
its learned reading of these things.

Night casually pencilled you in—
first some incidental shading, then
the dark edges of the page
edging their way to the centre.

Ceiling fan, Villefranche

In whose well-rounded company you might sleep
as soundly—pigeons, dervishes,
        a turbine or waterwheel

                installed on the ceiling.
A perfect circle the ear
recognises—flawless sigh

of a lettuce, drying
in a wire basket
        at the end of one long, swinging

                arm. Or the rotating
daughters of the Italian Navy, each morning
on the training ship *Berlusconi*

jogging in circles on the aft deck. Other
equally rehearsed details keep coming around—
        the ceremonial cutlasses, sprightly

                footwear and gelati,
uniformity of their nut-brown
bikinis. The eye returns to them

what is theirs; just as it keeps returning
to the ceiling fan above us—
        a spool

                around which
you and I, sleeping or awake,
are slowly unwound.

A consort of flower parts

for Jen

If the life of the mind is
a history of
interesting mistakes
        then what of

the life of the body—a memorable swim
within certain boundaries?

As in a botanical diagram,
letters are usually assigned
        the diverse parts:

stem, leaf, stamen, much the way
those same letters are dispersed
across the writerly sky
        above Hataitai.

So, too, our marriage was
annotated, inflected.
Let's go swimming, you said,
        in your blue shoes. Who needs

an ocean
or the blustery light

all about us. Afternoons
I returned to the suit
in which I was married,
        the blackness

of its incomparably blue
day—the sea of where it was
        we went.

8

It was us, alone,
but not for long—others joined in,
names were distributed,
commas placed between them,
    bedrooms added,
instruments assigned.
Chandeliers hovered above
our time together,

letters of a glass alphabet. We thought
the world. And how it was we came to be
who we were

    or just west of there.
In the coral sea you were
the brightest of fishes
    and I was marooned
half way through a poem called
'Beauties of the octagonal pool'.

There were, at times, differences
concerning music, the lifespan
    of a couch, number of books
on a shelf, the time anything

takes. The year the Australian
Prime Minister wouldn't say 'sorry'
    we made a picnic
of the cold

but you were nowhere to be found
on that icy rug. We had driven
    down a side road,
at the end of which
a sign: 'Sorry, Garden Growing'.

It was the comma, carefully rendered,
that held us—this comma at the end of
    Hokianga Harbour,
high above Omapere, an eyelash
        or falling star. The comma

after 'sorry'
which followed us south.
We thought the world

    of each other, and
beyond the bird-like lettering
    the cathedrals of
our time together
were a succession
    of photo-booths. Times
we forgot to smile.

It was Spring
or thereabouts
    and the high-flying punctuation
of Hataitai, all flower parts
and parts of speech, was
all about us. Out-of-service buses
bearing the word 'sorry'
    coasted by.

    With its dream of
perfectly spaced
events and objects, it is the comma
    that outlives these words—between

'sorry' and 'garden growing',
a seedling dropped
between adult plants. Whatever else
the season delivers

in the end all we have is
that
    which exists
between us, a pod and a curl,
which holds us
    together.

Line

Of being in love, it is said
one eye should remain
        fixed, the whole time, on

the horizon, the horizon being
an essential element,
        along with a street

directory, packaged lunch
and a scar—
        there always being

a scar
on one or other,
        even if it takes time

to find. The eye, thus engaged,
will always note the watery cicatrix
        left by a motorboat

or the line that follows two boys
dragging a branch
        along a beach. Such is also

the nature of a scar, but as for
its location; Love, as they say, that
you must find
        for yourself.

Love poem

Houses are likened to shoeboxes but shoeboxes are not
likened to houses. A car is likened to a heap but a heap is not
likened to a car. A child is a terror but terror is not a child.
A business might be a sinking ship but a sinking ship is no
business. A bedroom is a dog's breakfast but a dog's breakfast
is not a bedroom. A bad review might be a raspberry but a
raspberry is not a bad review. A haircut is likened to a disaster
but a disaster is not a haircut. Books can be turkeys but turkeys
are never books. A holiday might be a riot but a riot is not a
holiday. A garden might become a headache but a headache is
not a garden. I dream about you but you are not a dream.

Ode to fashion

for Doris de Pont

Of your over-reaching lines
and displaced
hems

enough said, fashion being
a kind of biography
in which

the shape of a life
is contained
but not

in words. Let us consider
instead what is revealed
in the measuring

room: the state of undress that lies
at the heart of dress. O
dizzying hemispheres

of Fashion, you encircle the
dangerous princesses
of Monaco

as you do the waists of young mothers
recently delivered of
their children.

Scholars listen to the rustling pages
of your collars and cuffs
as indeed they might ponder

the infinite sleeves
of your infinite arms
rocking us

both towards and away
from sleep. So like
and so unlike

the world of which you are
a part, you have
your designs

and your points of distraction
your deft marriages
and the occasional

embarrassment. Out on your limb
you wear your creases
but not as

we wear age. You are
also a museum
of gestures,

glances, with your multi-storied
wardrobes, those libraries of
previous seasons—

apartment blocks in which
evenings of a life
are stored.

If we tumble, your good skirts
will gather us
and if we fall

your lavish designs will raise us
again. Should we become
unstitched

your fabrics will wrap around the two
of us—at least until
season's end. Then

it will be
      curtains
and the wafting poetry
      of curtains
for you

floating out towards the horizon
of the infinity pool
where these

cultivated waters touch
a raging sea, that
quiet seam

beside which I sit
awaiting further
instructions.

The camera is a small room

The camera is a small room
large enough for you or me
but one of us
         will have to
stay outside. A small room
with a red hedge
bamboo grove
         and mirrored sun.
The camera is a

home for old people. A small country
where the inhabitants
         live simply
their long lives
pass swiftly. Trees grow
instantly to any size that suits.
The camera is a chatterbox
         of the eyes
a barge on the faintly etched
surface of the harbour.

An article of hope
         of fine weather
a brave new whirl
         its cool ripe visions
slowly digesting the snake-earth.

2. *The sea of where it was we went*

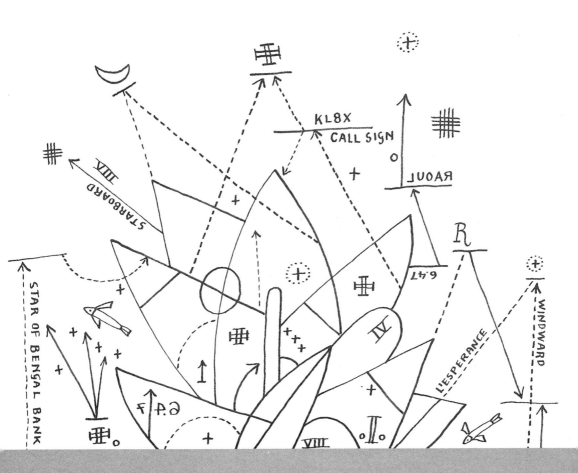

A guide to the frogs of Fiji

We were five days into
the month of fragile things

or so the ukulele kept reminding
us. A casual strum.

The village rooster out pecking
on the far reef.

What we didn't know we read
in a guide to the frogs

of Fiji: that, in late winter,
a soft, low-pitched trilling

crosses the moonlit golf course;
that males of a certain age

lack spines. What to look or
listen for:

'a soft coo-coo-coo like the sound
of a two-stroke

generator', 'a rising moan
repeated, softly',

a croaking to drown
the waterfront vows

of the newly-weds; the males
of the species ready and

available, but only in early spring or
following heavy rain.

19

A rattling window, Sigatoka

A great country should be governed as one would
cook a small fish, that is, not pulling it about.
—*Lao Tzu*

Mid-afternoon, the palms were all
windmills. A light southerly saw

to that. Half the village
half submerged

in the lagoon. We were taken by them
out beyond sea cucumbers and starfish

to discuss the virtues of good government,
the democracy of palms.

The glass-bottomed boat drifting above
or was it below us

contained only sky, frigate birds, the odd, hesitant
cloud. The palms, we were

captive to them. Taken, later, by foot and by Sunbeam
Bus Company to a great book

of a building—a bible chapel—we noticed
a t-shirt, a flag twitching in

what remained of the wind: *NADRO STALLIONS . . .*
GUIDED BY THE PRIEST (Matt. 6:33)

Seek ye first God's Kingdom and he shall
provide you with great things

in life: horses, rugby posts, trophies. A few doors down
from WESTERN WRECKERS LTD,

the Blue House Man had two storeys, the first held up
by soft-drink bottles. Such things as he told us

we were not to know—that the aloe vera plant
was two villages away, that a single leaf

might conceal an armed man (and he described for us
the firing mechanism of

a peacekeeper's rifle as though it were
a truly remarkable insect),

that the ukulele down the corridor at 5 p.m. was in fact
three villages away. And the *Rattling Window*

we caught from Sigatoka was now eleven villages,
a half an island, a wide world

away, leaving in its dust the great, crumbling wall
of Fiji, the island's silent alphabet

of coral—a beach laden with spanners, telescopes, compasses,
hammers, levers and forks—

instruments to repair a rattling window, to fine-tune
a fairer world.

Coral

The bamboo pavilion is remembered
but only for its lawn
of yabbering frogs. The lagoon

has already forgotten us, the smallest
brightest fishes disappearing
back inside the brain.

A swim, mid-ocean, upon reaching the Tropic of Capricorn

I remember it more
as a falling
or clambering

through mid-air, a
tussle
in which I was

made to wear a wide
blue hat.
What I lacked

in style
I made up for
in altitude.

This many days
from shore
and the body already

an ocean in which
the bones
drift. And the mind

an island tucked
beneath
its horizon. All that surrounded us

either bone or brain
and the free passage
of fishes in their midst.

A naval exercise (for two hands)

Six minutes is all you have
      to get the man overboard
back on board. A lifebuoy
      will be thrown, a boat
dispatched, one hand
      will comb the water with
a searchlight, another will man
      the shark-gun. All you have is
six minutes to bring him
      in—a few seconds more than
Purcell's 'Lord, what is man,
      lost man, that thou should'st be
so mindful of him' and two thirds
      the duration of John Adams'
'The Perilous Shore', which
      probably isn't what anybody
is wanting to hear just now. It is exactly
      the length of José Marín's
'No piense Menguilla ya' and of
      The Peddlers playing 'Girlie'
at a Martinborough vineyard; the same
      duration also as Pachelbel's 'Canon'
played at an appropriate tempo
      and with the necessary sense of a life
being saved, of living in a world
      where no one is ever lost.

The mechanical rat of Raoul Island

The first and last of his species
he comes to us

on four wheels, down an aisle
of banished trees

pawpaw, purple guava—an upturned
dinghy or wound-up

trinket, above whose royal grimace
the returning birds

wheel and glide—there to consider
the emptiness of these islands

and a sky filled to bursting:
the redundant king

of some far, disconsolate land.

An artist's guide to the layers of an ocean

The first as much a layer of sky
as it is a cloth

laid between islands and
across which nib

and quill manoeuvre
as if on a naval

exercise, passing directly above
the zone

of fugitive colours,
gouache and wash.

Ten metres down is the zone
of coloured inks
    and pastel fish

diving birds like brushes
or pencils plumbing

the depths. Further again—
beyond crayon and acrylic—

swimming through washes
of blue and grey, all manner

of fish-like flecks—yellow, gold
and green—

then, in the half light,
each painted canvas is
    a net laden

with ghost shark and
Kermadec rig, palette fish
    and plankton.

Further still—eyes of the signal fish
etched into hemispheres

of coral. And in this
the sea's darkest room

one fish is
a tripod, another

a pinhole camera, registering only
an ink blackness traversed by

ribbons of light and the
fountain-pen plumes

of undersea volcanoes. Here
in this last,

nocturnal zone, we recognise
the blue-black urchin—a satellite

lost in the darkness—
a wide open eye

that sees nothing
    but understands
all.

A mule, Raoul Island

As steep a track
by any other

means, we were
pushed and

prodded. This was how
our luggage

treated us. A meandering commentary
each corner of

the winding track. A reasonable
judgement

we expected of them—a sensible ratio,
of oranges to mules, that one

might not lose the path, as was sometimes
the case

for the less sure-footed
in our train—those for whom

sinking comes more naturally
than swimming.

There was patience to be learnt
emptying the orchard

at Fishing Rock—where we were once
ourselves offloaded

by hoist and derrick, raised up and rendered
freestanding

above the shark-hungry bay.
A mule records its days

in mileage, haulage,
whatever else

it has to offer: an innate sense
of volcanology,

seismology. Yet, in
times of unrest

we stood our ground
knowingly, as parakeets fled

to outlying rocks. An even temper in
the face of such tantrums

of earth and sea. The track wrapped
around us; we were contained

but not confined by
it. We were

packed and put upon
for as many years

as an orchard
could grow, to be finally

set free, replaced by
petrol engine

and flying fox, a loud wire.
In another life

we might have been
tropicbirds, in whose

nocturnal plumage we could make out
the forms of each oncoming day,

not so much as it approached, but as it
fell upon us,

our tails woven, well-packed
with stars and

moons, and these
our only burden.

Rangitahua

A dip in the alkaline crater-lake—ten minutes
and you will have lost
                    your fingerprints; ten minutes overboard
off Meyer Island and the fish life
will know you

        better than you know yourself; ten minutes in
last week's cyclone and the grapefruit tree
is stripped of every leaf, but the fruit,
untouched. The same ten minutes

it takes to empty the bagpipes of its music
before stepping on to a boat that reminds one Mr Bell
of an oversized stringed instrument.

Ten minutes is how long the twentieth century
lasted on Raoul Island, the time in a ghost net
it takes for dolphin and albatross to become themselves
        ghosts. Time enough

to say goodbye. Wattage of the flashlight fish
fading on deck.

Ode to Futuna Chapel

for Peter McLeavey and in memory of John Scott

By crumpled sea and
sloping horizon,

I came to the chapel of Futuna—
by overgrown path

and a circular garden described only
by thought.

It was the high tide
delivered me

from anemones, madrepores and
a haze of frigate birds

tattooed on the forehead of
St Peter Chanel.

In such details
my eyes were cast

adrift. Finally, I reached the chapel of Futuna
and described it thus:

a rock pool or cistern in whose waters
all things are set afloat. Here

I began my study of its diagonals, the dispensation
of grace, light toppling from

its many-coloured ceiling. A sky made
of watermelon, pomegranate and lime.

It was the smell of rhubarb boiling on a distant stove
that carried me this far

and held me here. Crab-footed, on the sea-bed
of this chamber, washed up

on the reef of
its altar

my hands were soon
swimming

between passages of brilliant
colour.

And I was not alone in this. It was
in the company

of diving birds, sunfish and
sargassum weed

that each of us became
a swimmer, each

in their own
solitude. Herein

we learnt
to swim.

∞

We arrived heavy with nouns, laden with
figures of speech

to sit under the heart pole, to linger
under the great tree, with its

foliage of blue and green. The yellow and
red of its floating leafage.

Equal parts concrete, wood
and light—that was the equation

33

we came up with for the chapel of Futuna, where
the two rows of pews formed

the shape of a capital L, this side of
the centre-pole—an umbrella shaft

reminding us of
a storm-tossed world

adjacent to this one, here
where the sun

is packaged and passed
from hand to hand,

where the angles of an
unsquare world

are made
square.

∽

Lagoon, or L-shaped
pool, in which the pews are

formations of waves—
such plans we had for your floor

this sea-bed on which we found ourselves.
The limitless sky

of it—this side of
the L-shaped afterlife.

Sunfish, moonfish, the earth
has many hands.

∽

To revisit your island of thorns, Futuna,
your crown of coral, this beach

on which the canoes
of faith and doubt

or any other vessel
are pulled ashore, and from which

they depart, well-laden.
I came

to the church at Futuna by way
of many wonders—

the native birds of Karori
that not only

imitate the ringing of a hundred
telephones, but have also

learnt from you
dawn's glassy silence.

I have seen an island the shape of
a gourd, a teapot with

two spouts and I have sighted your
disappearing Christ

in an updraft
above the albatross colony

at Taiaroa Head.

Paper swan, hibiscus flower,
you are the tail

of a bonito re-entering
the water, as southern

as any ocean. You are our
Sargasso Sea—

beneath the open book of
your architecture,

your hefty pages frozen
at the perfect moment

of their narrative. A star embedded
in the firmament,

you have the character of both shellfish
and stringed instrument—

you are a shelter or clearing
in which we find

our voices. And begin
to sing

our L-shaped hymns
in the L-shaped silence

of your body.

Richard Henry in Fiordland

The mind of man is nothing
but an aviary
                    the sodden book says
or so sang Richard Henry
in the company of
                    waterfalls, those thinnest
most radiant of men.

The roof over Richard Henry's head
          a roof of birds
and the ground beneath his feet
          his lightly feathered nest.
A world as full of birds as
          the minds of men.

When stoat weather took apart
the kakapo pen
                    Richard Henry swam
even deeper down, beyond feather star
and coral tree, his own species,
          a sea as empty of birds
as the sky above.

These amplified days, tui sing
from their shining box, these most
          unlistening of days,
hums Richard Henry, these
birdless days. And this
my birdless song.

Wet Jacket Arm

Was it a cap
made of thrum
or just the over-
hanging weather—

Richard Henry's 'fine
country for
the waterproof explorer'
or, as Cook noted, 'a densely

wooded head'. We came as far
as the end
of most things—Foot Arm
was only a body of water

away. The lengthening shadows
of a rainforest no longer there.
And even the mildest tea
sipped on the *Breaksea Girl*

would not sweeten
this pepper forest, nor
evening in its dusky coat
steady these unlevel waters.

A shift in the wind

Long-winded night
bragged on

and next morning
a window in

the weather. Starboard
the airy pavilion,

waterfalls like walking
sticks, the body

not much longer
for its rest.

Any moment
now.

The Ailing Wife

*'There was a new softness in the air . . .' wrote Malaspina,
approaching Doubtful Sound at the southwestern end of
New Zealand's South Island in 1793. He and Don Felipe
Bauzá, who explored Doubtful Sound in a rowing boat from
the corvette* Descubierta, *were responsible for the twelve
Spanish place-names in the area. While the first European
music heard in New Zealand is said to have been that played
by English sailors on fife, drum and pipes in 1773, the first
conceivable instance of a guitar being heard in the country
was when the two Spanish vessels of the Malaspina expedition
visited two decades later.*

Punta de 25 de Febrero

It was stained as the sea was
stained

tannin-brown. A wintry forest
of six strings.

Sweetness, she stood on the pier
and passed me

the guitar. And with that
I was pushed

out to sea. I sailed latitudes
of frets, longitudes

of strings. I worked on my hands.
My nails

grew, fingertips hardened
and, this way,

I was restrung.

Isla de Bauzá

So had it the talkative hands
with which I accompanied

myself. Slowly as we went
the instrument and I

out towards the horizon of
her ailment

that we might make
dry land again

on this ship I called
The Ailing Wife

sailing calmly for
the storm.

Islotes de Nee

The fair sea, she said,
the unfair sea . . . My wife had left instructions

for playing the instrument
in the foulest weather

come rain, typhoon or
waterspout.

But she had not prepared me for
the calmness, these wide

unmoving waters. Slowly,
as we went.

Canal de Malaspina

I clung to her. A lesson learnt from crayfish,
the left hand's shuffle

neck-wards. A lesson learnt
from sails:

that we are gathered
inwards. A thinness

she taught me. Slackness
I taught myself, and then

unlearnt it. J. S. Bach
you were

a bridge over the river
of such things.

Together we pressed onwards to
the upper reaches

of her sickness.
A lesson learnt

from gut strings:
a necessary tension.

Punta de las Marcaciones

Our two sons were
the Hare's Ears

outlying rocks on a
seaward passage

unamused by this or any
other ocean

all they could do to keep
their heads above the blackness.

Punta de Espinosa

Together we played the wind-tossed
waters of Wet Jacket Arm.

J. S. Bach, you held me as
many have been held

and kept from falling. Crayfish
and black coral

I also studied with them. Pinched
and plucked I was

taut, laid flat as
any island

above which music drifts. But still
I worked on my hands

tracing paths through this forest
of six disorderly vines.

Punta de Quintano

Not long after the arrival of
the pipes, fife

and drum, a Spanish guitar was
rowed up the fiord

45

Guerau's 'Poema Harmonico'
rendered appropriately

with its ties, trills, mordents
temblores,

afectos. We were likewise flying
the Spanish flag

despite a language we found increasingly
incomprehensible

and a labyrinthine tablature
perfectly in keeping

with this world
so far beyond us.

Puerto del Pendulo

Clouds were playing
'Wake me up

and send me home' upon
the water.

Sailed they then
The Ailing Wife
sailed they some.

Canal del Norte

Laid me down on a bed
of Luys de Narváez. From

inside the instrument my wife
listened. And when

the dark sea rolled
we rolled

as one. Laid me down
on a bed of

Francisco Guerau. Through the round
window of the instrument

she stared up at me.
Laid me down

on a bed of John Dowland.
But there was no dry land

ever again, only
the distracted sleep

of the unwell, and this
incessant sailing.

Canal del Sur

I studied my hands and where
they went

this delicately strung dwelling
its spine, ribs, a certain

breathed-in space, the hollow body
turning

these dolphin-besotted waters.

Cascada

Together we made our way up the neck
of the instrument

                this jumping-off
place. I had grown accustomed

to the fact you loved me less
but, perhaps, not

less well. I had climbed down
from the overhanging tree

            of my instrument,

packed my things, this guitar
already overgrown

gone back to native forest,
birdsong, lichen.

Atlas Montanas

J. S. Bach you reside here
and if I knock

            you answer. Not
in so many words, you make

room for me among
the crowded strings. All I can offer

in return: this parched
ocean, this undry land,

this place where I live
now. And if you knock
    I answer.

4. Red square, black square

Guests of the Rossiya Hotel!

The number of guests should not exceed the number of beds in a room.

The guests of the hotel are kindly requested not to disturb other guests, to keep quiet and follow The Social Order both in and outside the room.

Please acquaint yourself with the information of how to behave yourself in a fire.

The guests of the hotel are not allowed to leave visitors in the room in their absence.

The guests of the hotel are not allowed to keep animals, birds, reptiles etc. in the room.

The guests of the hotel are not allowed to keep huge and bulky things in the room.

In the rooms you can find forms where you can write your complaints and suggestions.

We suggest you make use of our barber shop.

Dear Guest!
Welcome to the 'Rossiya' Hotel

Woman sleeping in an art gallery

It is seldom enough—the way
a body is carried through a town

even if the snow is put to good
effect. And the six months' painting

in it. The Tsar and his family are always
facing the wrong way. But there is one painting

I sit well beneath: a Russian saint,
in one light-filled hand a potato, in the other

a billiard cue. My chair sings like a bird
as I adjust my weight beneath him. As

the world is balanced, I am
balanced. I close my eyes.

Outside Lenin's tomb

Neither amused nor transported by them
we fell amidst men with large hats

and even larger ambitions. One—ex-Red Army,
a dealer in reptiles—had installed

a family of iguanas and four-metre snakes around
the nearest pond. Who was going to argue

with that? Another tried to interest me in
the Helicopter-Christ on his wrist—

the minute and hour hands spinning at the tip
of a Byzantine nose. I had

neither faith nor time. A hundred roubles,
another said, to be photographed

with either or both of his monkeys, or a falcon
on your shoulder. With rain

approaching from the south, he then offered
all of the above

for said price—with Comrade Lenin thrown in.
In danger of sobering up, the look-alike, with red party ribbon,

black suit and cap, must have thought the chances
of another drink were dwindling,

the weather, like the twentieth century, having
not turned out exactly as planned.

Rain had already sent the reptiles back inside
their manager's clothes, the biggest snake

slipping beneath the pond water; a sleeve came down
like an overcast day on the Helicopter-Christ

as we crammed the foyer
of the Russian church.

The sunflowers had turned blue
with cognac and cellphones were playing

polkas. From the hotel at the end
of the square, Marx, Putin and the Last Russian Tsar

were now gesturing to Lenin; someone had
clearly come upon

a bottle of something. And then
above the square of the red-faced

and uncertain of foot: the words of Lenin

advancing between gusts of rain, addressing
the children of this or any other

revolution: Let us hold close that which
we still have:

reptiles, a hawk, two monkeys and
the tears of the Russian presidents

as they fall upon the Russian presidents,
no longer recognising them.

Words sung by a Russian soprano

for Masha Zheltova

Not as I listen to them or as you might sing them
but as, much later, we walk with you

across a frozen river. A Russian song
is never less than that. A ledge

just inside the ear on which music like melting
snow is stored. Which is why

I study your mouth so precisely: to gauge
the shape of each word—

and what accompanies it:
the keyboard

a ladder up to your voice,
a wind-blasted steppe

upon which we stand
and fall. But the song upholds

the singer, just as birdsong
does the bird

on its rickety bough,
high above

suitcase and shovel, the sinking
cathedrals of this world.

Rublyov

Cathedral of the Saviour and Andronicus

Truth was the circle we drew around it.
Andrey, I have heard it said

your church stands at an unlikely angle
to history. And that summer here

has a comparable intelligence—poplars
shedding their fine, unseasonal snow

of brotherhood, love and reconciling faith.
'The ground upon which I fall

is Christ.' You once addressed this
improbable world, arranging

burnt twigs in snow. 'These lines are only
an arrangement of birds

flying.' These we loose
like kites above the tundra

that they too might be allowed their moment,
that they, too, might depart.

Black square

What lasts. A faded yellow taxi pulls up outside the Hotel Rossiya
—a vast structure scheduled for demolition in the new year—then
drives off with two Americans and three suitcases. That was eighteen
months ago. The four-door sedan has outlived the three-thousand-
room edifice.

∾

As though it were a life-raft to keep them afloat during the
uncertain times ahead, the local population gather around the
periphery of Red Square. It is early evening and the turrets and
domes of the Kremlin have about them the air of a shipwreck.

∾

For pilgrims of modern art, however, the true centre of Moscow
has never been Red Square. It is Kazimir Malevich's *Black Square*
(1915), hung high on a wall of the New Tretyakov Gallery.

∾

The Mona Lisa of Modern Art, as the *Black Square* is sometimes
labelled; it has also been described as the icing on the cake of early
twentieth-century experimentalism. Black icing on a very black
cake, as some doubtlessly said at the time of its creation.

∾

With this painting very much in mind, I arrive in Moscow and,
having hiked the 300 corridors of the Hotel Rossiya, pull back the
covers on my single bed to find something lodged between pillow
and sheet. What looks at first like a Malevichean black square turns
out to be a neatly folded woman's negligée.

∾

Not knowing whether the placement of said garment is a Russian tradition or—more worryingly—if someone has already checked in to the room, I transfer the lacy item to the adjacent table. I check the wardrobe for other clothing, but there is none. Then the bathroom. The brand name on the label of this exceptionally transparent garment is, I note, *JENNI Lingerie*.

∾

If this had happened during the Soviet era, the negligée might have been construed as a veiled threat.

∾

The name of my wife is Jennifer.

∾

Somebody must know something.

∾

Holding the negligée up to the window and looking through it, the city of Moscow appears as in an old grainy photograph. Draping it over the back of the only chair in the room, I wonder if the hotel cleaners will remove this paradoxical garment—at once black and transparent—when they service the room in the morning.

∾

Twice, not long after checking in, my telephone rings and a woman's voice says, in faltering English, that if there is anything at all I require, *not* to go to the hotel reception but to come instead to room such-and-such on the fourth floor. Accordingly, a mysterious narrative begins to assert itself, involving the telephone, a great many corridors, the black negligée and the city beyond.

∾

The morning after my arrival, when I finally find myself standing in front of Malevich's *Black Square* at the Tretyakov, I cannot dislodge the black negligée of the Hotel Rossiya from my mind.

∞

Black Square appears much less absolute in real life than it does in reproduction. The canvas looks as though it must have spent the past eighty years stashed behind a filing cabinet—which may well have been the case during the Soviet era, when it was seldom seen and was probably regarded as a manifest lapse in the collective socialist consciousness. Far from the pristine, resolute painting encountered in books, the canvas resembles a segment of the Russian steppes viewed from an aeroplane: all cracks and rivers and flooded valleys, moonlit.

∞

Leaving the gallery, I notice I am being followed by an ice-cream vendor who is pushing what appears to be a refrigerator laid out on a set of wheels requisitioned off two children's bicycles. An antiquated outboard motor attached to the rear generates a suitably Russian frostiness for the man's wares. The man is wearing sunglasses, the lenses of which are two black almost-squares. These give him the appearance of either a blind man or a KGB agent, or both. The year-round popularity of ice cream among Muscovites is, I am later told, a matter of civic pride—as if the substance afforded a kind of mystical union with their icy continent; the white orbs of ice cream raised like communion bread above endless snowy expanses or grey pavements.

∞

The cleaners have not removed the black negligée.

∞

One of the great lessons of the Kremlin cathedrals is how indebted Russian avant-garde art—with its black crosses, circles, squares and flattened space—is to the tradition of icon painting. Malevich's black square could have been lifted from the garment of any of a great number of saints.

∞

At least as prominent as the squares and crosses in this city of squares and crosses is the onion dome—a form perfectly calibrated so that no snow can gather upon it. Hence the commonplace utterance: 'We must be as onions upon which the snow of this world falls.' Alleviated from such load-bearing, the onion domes of Moscow are destined to outlast even the city's crosses, rectangles and the black and red squares.

∞

Checking out of the Hotel Rossiya three days after my arrival, I consider packing the black slip into my suitcase. Then I imagine being held up at the airport, the contents of my bag emptied. And being marched down a lengthy corridor to where my accusers would await me.

∞

A short distance from here, in the Kazan Cathedral, a young man, his eyes unaccustomed to the light, snags the black veil of a devout young woman with his sunglasses. I wheel my suitcase out into the darkening square. Its mystery unresolved, the negligée is left folded in a neat black square.

∞

At the time of writing, the shiny kilometre-long rectangle of the Hotel Rossiya is being demolished, room by room, unpicked like a massive knitted jumper. The authorities have decided not to use explosives lest they cover the entire city of Moscow in a layer of dust. Demolition proceeds not only with the precision of dentistry but with a good number of government agents in attendance to deal with security issues: to cover up traces of the network of Soviet-era tunnels which led from the hotel to the Kremlin and as far away as the city's Garden Ring Road. These indefatigable figures also busy themselves pocketing what remains of at least three thousand clandestine listening and looking devices and any other incriminating remnants of an overly attentive earlier world.

What lasts. Stumbling atop these piles of fresh rubble, the Russian agents chase the black negligées as soon as the wind picks them up. But there are not enough agents and soon a cloud of black silk is drifting beyond the half-demolished hotel, across the Kremlin ramparts and high above the ornate domes of recently reconstructed cathedrals.

5. Little Oneroa

Little Oneroa

In the seaward room, all windows,
they had accomplished something
with peas

a light green paste on which
a fine percussive seasoning
had fallen.

Islands of summery bread were
summoned and an explanation
offered concerning

the use of lemon peel as a
navigational aid.
So began

my apprenticeship
in such matters.
Of the rain

only footnotes remained: a
ceramic fountain, a drink
knocked over

by a pukeko. And to close formalities
the chef's final offering—
a running rabbit.

Sprig

Nelson, site of the first game of
rugby played in New Zealand, 1870

Here, according to this plaque
the egg was laid
                    only a grubber
or chip kick from the exact centre
of the country—

                    one wet, running
afternoon played, without
exaggeration, in swimmers and
polished shoes—a town, smallish

by degrees, the winner on
the day the light between trees
a green cushion
                    on which a tight head

might rest, a whistle blowing
down the years
                    the oval egg
dreaming its bright bird
the scrum pressing onwards
            to its Byzantium.

A fall of ice on Mt Maunganui, 11 May 2009

Having seen everything
we look for something
less—lightning farms

of Bethlehem, snow-stopped
sea off Papamoa, the baffled minds
of avocado and men.

On shelter belt and More FM
a snow-like falling—
on television news and

migrant labour; on Gloria's
orchard, truckloads of white
unseasonal fruit.

And the tractor that
has never before shined
just so.

A small ode to faith

for Bill Manhire

Seated, as we were, eleven rows
    inside the hungry belly

        of the faithful, our religion was
fishing. And it was our religion

        made us fishermen. We were ushered
        down the long aisle of

a pier, at the end of which murmured a vast
        green harbour. Between

        a bucket of slop and the entangled talk
of a dozen water-logged men

        we professed all that we now clove to:
        the fish with piano accordion gills

stirring in an orange bucket
        the detachable heads of trumpeter

        and damselfish, blenny, spotty
and leatherjacket. It was not

        their small minds we were drawn to
        but their shining fuselage

held like a pen in one hand—a model
        proposed for us: well-schooled, and rendered

        in great detail, expelled from their
natural element

their aloneness. You must be fishers
        of men, we were told, with our alphabet of

hooks, lexicon of sinkers, lures
and spinners. While down the non-fishing end

    of things
        under-sized boys kept

throwing themselves back, we
    made of this

        our pier-bound profession:
the backward somersaults of faith

        beyond tide table and filleting board
           where a factory ship lingered

like the Church of Scotland, emptying its icebox into
    the midsummer sea. Deep in this

        thicket of rods, these faithfully
           rendered waters

with our next-to-nothing fish
    and meagre vocabulary

        our fishing only a dream

of swimming,
a chimney of birds
    to smoke the fish king

        and being rescued.

The Surfers' Mass

One believes in the other—
the awakening body

the soul's repose—that you have to
stand up so as to

fall down. Five p.m. at Saint Michael's
a trap best laid

after a weekend's swell, saltwater lakes
on the pews beneath our

boardshorts, a trail of sand as far as
communion—

we were carried in and washed
back out.

God above all: Fiona's birthmark,
Mary-Louise's Sunday

shoes, and Bernadette come lately from tennis
seen through

a veil of incense. Moira of the Roman
sandals. It confirmed us

in our doubt. Afterwards, the cup of tea
in the crypt, then walking home

on footpaths that extended
beyond description

the wandering mind catapulted out
into the early evening

certain that God's love would never give out
on us, as brittle

and enduring as an afternoon's tennis
played with Bernadette or

Mary Shanahan until
the bitter end.

The non-singing seats

*in memory of Maxwell Fernie, who from the church
organ, conducted the choir at St Mary of the Angels,
Wellington, for forty years until his death in 1999*

It was air that gave the grand thing
life. Like a sailboat

or newborn, it was sprung
to song, drawing us up

the encircling staircase
to its loft

where the choirmaster directed
his forest of pipes.

You should sing as though running down
a grassy slope,

we were told, and here it was
our three sons drifted

gull-like, amidst the rackety cylinders,
and came to know this world

by measures. We were all ears,
aloft, and this way,

mouths firmly shut, we were taught
to sing—Max's head

a rising sun above
the keyboard

feet as busy upon the pedals
as a pedestrian

taking Allenby Steps
two at a time.

Mid-song, I would lift my children
so high

above my head they became
the tallest people

in the world. And so it was,
we were, and will remain,

running down a green slope
towards a town called

Palestrina or Johann Sebastian
or simply an outline

of Wellington airport
embalmed in fog,

planes unable to land
and us, the chosen few

about to lift off.

Silver gelatin print, Russell, Bay of Islands

for Laurence Aberhart

Given, as taken, from a westward-leaning wharf
trailings of rust buckets,
                              evening ferries. And, later,
a sheet of photographic paper adrift in the windowless room.
There is only one fish in the sea.
                              Many times over.

6. Among trees

On hearing, at the Oceanographic Museum, Monaco, the outcome of the New Zealand elections, November 2008

The silvery Lookdowns (Selene vomer) *disappear in the dazzling surface reflection as they slide through the water like blades . . .*—Guide to the Oceanographic Museum

There were fishes somehow
set apart

the silver surface of them
shining

but not necessarily as we would have
this world shine.

We had retired to the royal aquarium
for some understanding

of recent developments, there to behold
these long-faced

fishes, the remote coinage of
their scales.

There were species we might have preferred:
one fish a decorated shoe, another

a stopwatch; one school
of thought was

a chandelier, the next
a regatta.

But it seemed, instead, we had chosen the silver
fish in its splendid isolation—

a banker in his private
vault—to whom might pass

the governance of underwater cities, this side
of the unfathomable weed.

Marseilles Fish Market

'A profound creek trickles down
to the indifferent ocean'—
          this way the guidebook

adjusts the view. When you buy a fish
you are procuring a chart of
many oceans. A fishing boat hardly

scratches the surface. A light breeze
          idles market-wards, trailing
the morning fleet, the Mother of All

above all
on her hilltop, fumbling clouds
          but holding fast

the fish-child. Dolorosa,
the shipwreck on your head
speaks to me

and while the crusaders are remembered
for bringing soap
          and the Greeks

for introducing olives, your fishermen
are remembered daily
          but only for
the morning's catch. For each of us

you would prescribe
the healing properties of a harbour
the restorative power
          of a sea voyage,

a long night's sleep and,
at dawn, posters pasted
to the side of every building

and to one motor-scooter
left overnight outside the Tonic Hotel.
Our lady of this

and that, were we to lose faith
we would find you on your throne
of salad leaves, in every alcove

of the citrus church, there to be
reacquainted with your silence
and all that has speech:

      the grass as it sometimes grows,
the avocado as it falls,
the sea, the roof over our heads.

Octopus

Oil, garlic, ink—this much
we have learnt:

that the smells of a town
are its intelligence,

that the inside of day
is night, and the interior

of an octopus is a
fishermen's chapel

or an unopened umbrella, wrestled
from the harbour floor

then, by a pair of tattooed
hands, turned

inside out. Early
afternoon

the fisherman himself turns
inwards, trousers billowing

above a balcony, outside-in—
pockets flailing

above the octopus-blackened
pavement, the day's labour

over, dealt with; as everything
outside as well as

inside the octopus
ends.

Among trees

after Umberto Saba

Art being a form of inaccuracy
the fountain stands
uncorrected, just west of
the orchestral hedge. Here too
we have added a lighthouse

but not for the navigation
of men—a water feature with
clamorous repertoire,
beneath which the old anxieties
gather like untuned guitars
with no one to play them.

The mayor of Sault contemplates the Mistral

With its curves and crumbling
extremities,

the road remains, as ever,
undecided—

the wind, on the other hand
is both a test of the town's character

and its defining character. A man soon forgets
where he is from

but the wind never
leaves home. Constant

on its window-sill or
ruffling a field

of lavender; it is also
an essential ingredient

in the local nougat—
a cherry-flavoured

rectangle of world-renown. Whereas
the criminals

of this town are lacking
motivation, and our cyclists

too recreational, the wind has been known
to repair a car, to dissect

a carcass. So, despite the vilest murders
being ascribed to it, we count the wind

among our more stately
citizens. It will drink

a glass of red wine with
the least of us.

Perched on its hillside, the village
is open to

suggestion. But we cannot leave yet,
the clocktower replies.

Our senior residents have only just
arrived: the lemon-coloured

Citroën, the rhinoceros beetle . . .
we must wait

another century. The town pretends
not to listen. The wind says, jump.

Rue Obscure

Dishes were being washed and plates cleared
in the restaurant beneath

the road. The waiter stared up at us
as though we were balloonists—

as we ourselves were always staring
upwards, to an underworld we imagined

high above. All of us caught in
the same perpetual updraft.

From the depths of the kitchen, the chef reached
skywards to serve the diners

overhead. So it was his finest recipes took flight—
in summer the lightest

meals propelled by the subtlest
breezes. In winter, the menus advancing

into the snow, knowing that
the dishes

would follow them.

Reading Italian poetry at Waihi Beach

for Vincent Moleta

A chestnut or cricket ball
it bounces

along the edge
of the known world

the well-tempered avocado
the well-trained satellite

hovers in the mind
before re-entry, then lands

on the orchard road
amidst a flock of well-heeled quail,

for whom waits
the patient motorist.

Geography of Northern Italy

An orchestra of
missing parts

Enrico's band of
olive trees, the
notes played

and the day's walk
between them.

Lamp

Because the light we need
comes in as many shapes

as that same light falling
upon your face, or shuffling

from tile to hexagonal tile, we move
in the exceptional company

of lamps—one like a comet or flare
cast high among the constellations and

bouquets that paper these walls. A tall lamp
stands like a man on the brink

of something; another is a pot of
black ink, or a milk bottle

filled with coloured stones. Yet another
has the word C A S I N O playing

upon it. Elsewhere the light proceeds
as instructed, falling amidst the lives

that define it, or is sadly
diminished, as when someone sits down

with a book, this book, and the pages are
one by one extinguished.

Ode to thought

Each was handed a toy yacht. Each was
       destined for the windward end

           of the pond. Such was
              the thinking, thought being

           the boat that sets the lake in motion, the child running
around the perimeter.

There to sail. And so
       each learns to amend or adjust his

           waterish ways—in the morning park
              where even the youngest head is polished

           by thought, as indeed the eyes are
by what they have seen

and what they have
       never seen. It is thinking which leads us

           by Ferris wheel or chariot,
              paternoster or by way

           of the Temple of Higher Thought back
to the inscribed ceiling

inside the head, the spiral staircase
       down which each thought

           clambers. Glamorous, seasonal,
              holding the light to best

           advantage, the human head
might at once appear fruit-like—or

carved from a rare or common
    vegetable, and placed, accordingly, at the very centre

        of the composition. Who would have thought?
          With you firmly in mind, noticing also

        a preoccupation with clouds, billowing drapes,
    tropical birds. And the danger that, at any moment, thought

might be usurped by its more attractive
    French aunt, nostalgia. Elsewhere,

        the human head must compete with the vase
          as an object of beauty, research,

        probability—what immense spaces
    are summoned forth—this head

upon which inappropriate or inadmissible
    hats have been placed.

        Armies might have marched before it
          or on its account . . . And the snow

        above and below every thinking
    and unthinking

thing . . . A flying machine or other such contraption
    might land or hover there.

        What else lurks beneath the marble
          forehead, the inscrutable dome? All manner

        of improper thinking or thoughts—
    an apartment block, a woman, lost in thought,

beholding herself in a Polish
    mirror . . . Who is responsible for this?

And what were they thinking? An act
        of errant thoughtlessness or just another instance

of thought as it is handed down to us
from our friends in high places, the clouds—

the earth's brains, as they
        are sometimes thought of. You don't need to look

        far to find a suggestion of the human head
            in the middle of everything—precisely etched or

rendered by a blunt pencil, as if
in fog. At times a head might be

a target. Was that a woman's
        shoe? A slim volume of verse? Could someone explain

        that thin, impetuous shadow
            moving at speed? Or, out on the quivering pond

        where two thoughts are jostling for windward
advantage, replacing one another until at last

both are replaced by another thought
        entirely. The phrase 'I have been thinking

        about you' could never just be
            just an afterthought. Or 'I was not thinking

        straight'—as if a yacht would ever take
the direct route across this

or any pond. I think
        not. The direction of thinking having taken us

        thus far, on its circuitous route,
            on this November morning

when the head of each man and woman
entertains only one encompassing thought:

a woollen hat and scarf, buttoned coat
the play of snow upon
those things

that snow
plays upon.

Paris–Berlin, 23 November 2008

7. *Romantic voyage*

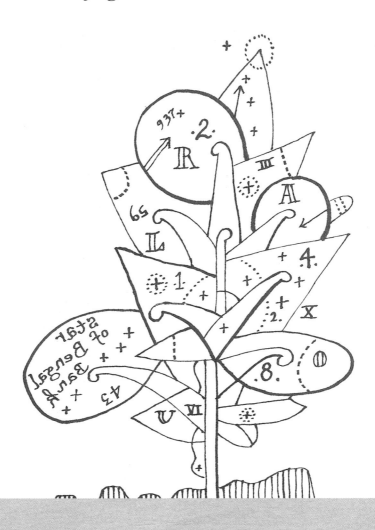

Solidarity with the anchovy

for John Jenkins and Ken Bolton

Are you listening, brothers?
There are consolations

though your daughters
are far from flashy, your sons

washed up and your long summers
confined to the icebox

women's stockings await you, fishnets
to lift you

out of your depths. You brave oceans
your only defence the way

you hold yourselves. Which is why
you are worth more than

your salt. And why
I address you midstream

this ocean a vast movie
starring each of you.

You dip your noses in black ink
and write the history of the world

page after unsullied
page. Maybe I am dreaming

but you shine
as dreams do, dug

like coal from pitch-black
ocean. You are

without contradiction
even if both violin bow

and fuselage of jet plane
have so obviously been modelled

on you. Or so you would argue
if argument was in the anchovy's

nature. Certain things you will never
understand: staircases,

traffic lights, the fourth draft of the poem,
much that lies beyond us

as well: Why a cellphone will never be
a celeste, even if a car horn

might one day become
a trumpet

played at the end of time
and, hopefully, well.

In houses by the sea we seek
your company, or some proximity

to your nocturnal
navigations. This we

agree upon, as four fishes in a flat tin
are in accord

and as they were once collectively seduced
by blinking lights and fishnets,

hauled upwards into
the opaque air.

Like instruments in a case,
your careers are streamlined—

you simply follow your nose,
your future

secure, preserved in salt
in oil you are professed,

blessed by the saint on the lid as
it is peeled back—heads down,

souls intact. I wrap this sheet
around you, this sheet

which is wrapped around
the both of us. Do you read me?

A moa-proof garden, Onehunga

for Michael Shepherd

A yard of sullen ancients. Dour
bivaricated clusters.
Spinifex.

What they lacked in green
was made up for
in canniness

buds tucked strategically inwards
leafage sprouting only
above the reach

of an adult moa. A garden given entirely
to burrs and spikes,
protective formation

of tightly wound hairnet or a
bagpipes from which
the airy music

had been extracted. We weren't
dressed for this: a chilling
updraft from

the Manukau Harbour, on the far side
of which 300,000 newly planted
natives

stood to attention. Between captain's
house and widow's walk—
monuments

to a lesser, human patience—we ascended
the skeleton of a modernist
house which was also

a great bird. In the empty room of the sky
above the harbour
we listened

to the dun-coloured garden ticking
beneath us, intent on
outlasting

our Japanese imports, gated communities
and Latin definitions. If we fell
from this twilit

balcony, the grove might catch
but would not
save us.

Letter to Louise St John, editor of
an anthology of New Zealand letters

Louise, I wanted to write
      one of those letters that begins
'I have been riding horseback
all day' or 'It's great
      to be back' or 'Hello, sweetheart
         I am trying to write this

in the bath. I have done
      a lot of crazy things
in my life but have never
attempted this before.'
      But your book kept
         interrupting me—and set me

thinking what exactly it is
      we send through the post:
gladness, pessimism,
a sense of family, or where we are
      precisely in this universe of
         wrong addresses and insufficient

postage. A friend of ours
      is always sending unwrapped
objects through the mail:
last week a stamped, addressed
      tennis shoe, this week
         a packet of seeds. Chris Cochran

once mailed our son Felix a leaf,
      forty-cent stamp affixed
and the address written carefully
upon it. Such miracles of
      the daily post—the infamous live eel
         inserted in the mail box at Opoutere.

Your next project should be *The Penguin Book of*
        Parcels and their Contents. Last year
prior to our return from France
I mailed 45 kg of books home
      filling our three-year-old's pushchair
          with bundles wrapped

in brown paper then trundling them down
        to *La Poste*. Along the way
I was met by suspicious glances
from neighbours who
      must have thought—with
          my poussette stacked child-high—

I was about to mail our well-wrapped
        three-year-old back to New Zealand.
On much earlier afternoons
my brother and I would
      march in single file
          out the kindergarten gate with

letters to our parents pinned to our backs.
        The glare from the flapping white sheets
attached to the children in front
of us: that was how letters
      entered our lives, and stayed.
        Have you ever considered editing

The Penguin Book of Lost Mail? 300 blank pages.
        Which brings us to other burning issues
of the day: war, pestilence
'has Harris watered the willows
      & planted my pumpkins & moved
          the bees', and whether we are losing

our attentiveness to language. Think
      of what, in the computer age, has happened
to the word 'attachment'.
I'm on the side of paper, Louise.
      This side. Which means I'm
        resolutely *with* your book

101

and with Frances Hodgkins' friend D. K. Richmond
  who always wrote in pencil
distrusting the newfangled
technology of
  the fountain pen. I'm for
   the Imperial typewriter

the word-processor, in moderation. If
  I have any complaints about your book:
D'Arcy Cresswell, who was more
successful as a blackmailer than a poet
  is under-represented, as are
   blackmailers in general. Yet another

time-honoured literary tradition
  the parking infringement notice
isn't given the time of day, neither
are the bills that cram
  our post box each morning. Rejection
  letters. Real estate flyers.

Perhaps you are already working on
  The Penguin Book of Junk Mail.
'The days run away', Louise.
I'll try to keep up with them
  ambling home around Oriental Bay
   your book in my backpack

all the letters contained therein
  rubbing against my shoulders
as though pinned there.
And I am back again
  at the kindergarten gate
   one in a long line

of children, one letter of an alphabet
a trail of punctuation marks
  dissembling up the street.

Dylan Thomas (b. 2003), Coolmore Stud, New South Wales

From a paddock lately nuzzled
by Groom Dancer, Pensive Mood
        and Pursuit of Love
the Welsh poet refinds his feet

belly filled with the green grass
of races
        freshly won, stable-mates consigned
to an adjacent pasture—Rock of Gibraltar
        Spinning World
and the self-harmer Tale of a Cat
chomping on stones,

Our Aristotle gone uncharacteristically
quiet, closer by the rowdy pavilion
        chewing silently
the silent, rock-strewn field.

Three elegies

1. Printmaking studio, Island Bay, Wellington

    for John Drawbridge

If ink were a city then I imagine
canals

      needle-boats, these rained-on
and half-remembered evenings

and the island a crushed hat
on a polished bench.

      If these lines were
a harbour, then I imagine night

as a great many swimmers
crosshatching the surface—

ink of their hands
hemispheres of their brows.

Your seaward house—
the intelligence

      of its windows, doors
in morning light—

we row the long boat of memory
out past forgetfulness, the island

a folded paper hat
you wear

          into the brightness
of each day

as it breaks, these quietly voiced
and barely registered mornings

in the next room
the night room now

down the long corridor
of your eye.

2. Low cloud, field of peonies, Martinborough

for Louise St John

Sleepless night
in your house

under the horizon—tiles
of an unfinished roof

sky of unfalling
leaves—you hold tightly

what you can: a farmer might lose
a paddock, a house disappear

down its staircase. This morning
knee-deep in fog, how it is

the peonies turn
their most avid reader

so suddenly
from their field.

3. Tangi, Parihaka

for Te Miringa Hohaia

Everywhere a voice
is heard—
          not this voice, but

the hollow back-bone
of a dog, or a volcano
breathing inwards.

Somewhere a sprig,
stem or root, a wreath
          worn in the hair
and the river
which is only as deep
          as the sky

and the coiled eel
its foundation stone.

Elsewhere a voice
not this one
          a beaten drum
in a flax basket—the heart
in its retiring place.

Around the head of each
an encircling greenness—
          karaka, karakia, these
expertly woven branches
          and leaves
that cannot hold him
                    to us

          but neither will they
          let him go.

Romantic Voyage

We took the No. 12 to some place
then the 14
        somewhere west
of there

       this deep in the flowery grass

we gave up waiting
for the No. 5
and took the 23

       the crickety mound where the season sings

having missed the No. 3
which was early
       we managed to catch
the 15
which was late
and took us as far as

      one green island, one gas tank, graffitied

that much accustomed place:
the outermost edge
      of things.

8. The invisible fathers

The invisible fathers

for Denis O'Connor

If I gave you nothing else, he said,
I gave you
    a roof over your head.
The sort of answer to the sort of question
we would have thrown our Irish fathers: What does the snow know
    about snowing. Or the clenched fist
of what it holds. And was it winter
or was winter
what you left behind.

Skills learnt on the violin applied to guns

There was something of that
in the leaving

    or the reasons
left behind. A tenacity born of ploughing
applied to the High Seas. Theirs was

a long afternoon at the far end
    of the quieting day
laid on their backs, creaking
like dinghies. Oars tucked
    neatly inside. White paint visible

under the blue.
    At the far end of the long bay
    of fatherhood.

A sea tune

We sat on the crabgrass, one in a dressing gown
another a life jacket
one on crutches, another bearing a tray
while the fifth bore a dinghy on his back
and appeared to be going nowhere in particular.
The visible fathers.

Inheritance

That part of you that is, he would say,
a man carrying a chair
          across a room. Such talk
being his way. Or a man carrying a reading lamp.
A man sleeping under a brass instrument.
          And that other part of you
which is none of these things.

Entering the home straight

It was Little Oneroa
          Blackpool
                    Little Oneroa
                              gaining ground. Stony Batter
finishing strongly on the inside. Ostend
falling off the pace. Onetangi
still a contender. Matiatia Bay
on the outside and down the home straight. Blackpool.
Little Oneroa. Onetangi
          fading fast. Blackpool.
                    Little Oneroa.
                              Matiatia Bay by a nose.
A nose, a neck and three lengths.

112

But it was not set in stone

Ours is a coastline of
wandering dunes, he said. And a *hopping dune*
      can be seeded by
as small a thing as
      a pebble. The sand, like a family
gathering around.

Familial

Fatherhood a museum of optics
      hall of mirrors: the smaller you get
the bigger you become.
      Our sons the oldest people
in the room, their lives extending furthest
      into the future. And
our daughters have become archaeologists
      of a world so dizzyingly far
          above us.

Home Strait

Long-winded summer
bragged on

Rathcoola to Kohimarama, Great Blasket Island
to Little Oneroa:

If I gave you nothing
I gave you

      the Stately Houses
of Orakei, the mainland off which

those of us float
    who can still float

or in whose nature
floating might be

in this most Irish
of seas.

Threnody

Seldom the dying—
it is the living darken
the day. A dying man walks
to the running sea.

Between voyages

A dexterity acquired
in the pit

applied to dance-floor
or morning harbour

our fathers, exiled from their
former selves, glided

marriage-wards, as lightly
as stones or shells

skimmed across water.

Antipodean

I put this to your father, Emmett,
        that Waiheke Island was
a replica of the Emerald Isle
rotated 90 degrees. An old shed

propped up by the sound
of an ocean on which
        until a moment ago
seven vessels were moored

and this poem
was one of them.

Days on earth spent

Listening to the roof slates
a man sleeping the deep sleep
of a brass instrument

all the spume-flecked day
his chisel a long boat traversing
the night waters of the stone.

Pilots

Beyond the violins and race-cards, it was the swimming—
our fathers, their hats still on, half way across
the creaking waters, the waves at Palm Beach calling
the 1.20 gallops from Ellerslie. An uncharacteristically
excellent result posted above the counter at Onetangi.

From the box of most things

At the end of his life
he had reached the end

of his father's tie
a further life's journeying

to circumnavigate
his father's hat.

The visible sons

One's feet dangled mid-air
another played the goat while
the oldest mastered the birdcalls
of species that had never reached
these shores.

Sadly, with fortitude.

One wrestled a chair while
the youngest stood atop the house
as though it were a ship of state
a pilot, like his father
untucked shirt and school tie
to steer by.

A seaward glance

If they left the world
it would be by long boat

and by long boat
be brought back.

Untitled

He of his father's eyes

He of his father's voice

He out of earshot of his father

He of his father's way with words

He of his father's indifference

He of the immense detail of his father's hands

He of the rain that falls from
    his father's head to his hands

He of the occasional crashing sound
    from the far corner of the empty house

He of the rain that falls from
    his son's head to his hands

He of the immense detail of his son's hands

He of his son's indifference

He of his son's way with words

He out of earshot of his son

He of his son's voice

He of his son's eyes

Islandmen

Down the home straight, the invisible fathers
were on the pace
       the coal-black horses

clamouring beneath them; the churchless fathers
who crammed
       both choir-loft and public bar

with their singing; in the courtroom
of their pleading
       their only defence

a range of herring-bone jackets and a few dance-steps
learnt in a mine
       by helmet-light and waving

a race-card; the winged fathers on their perches
tarred and
       bird-feathered; the absent fathers

long 'gone upstairs'
in their borrowed suits

the dance-floor or harbour they once crossed so lightly
the field mowed,
       the boat rowed.

Afternote

After two decades away, I have lately found myself returning to the city of Auckland and environs. The Waitemata Harbour is the 'octagonal pool' in this book's title—although a sideways glance is also cast to the courtly paintings of Jodhpur India. I've often wondered what shape Auckland's harbour occupies in my mind. It's definitely not rectangular, but neither is it round; 'octagonal' feels about right.

Part of this eight-part, or octagonal, book is made up of remembered vistas, predominantly from an Auckland youth; other poems travel widely in space. Some were commissioned for a diverse array of contexts—from the launching of Doris de Pont's Winter 2006 fashion collection to the celebration of an anthology of New Zealand letters. 'Sprig' was published in the *New Zealand Listener* during the 2007 Rugby World Cup. 'Dylan Thomas' was commissioned by Sydney-based painter Noel McKenna for an exhibition in the Hunter Valley in May 2010. Not only was the poem incorporated into various of Noel's paintings, it was embroidered on to a horse blanket which was worn by a thoroughbred at the opening. 'Richard Henry in Fiordland', 'A shift in the wind' and 'Wet Jacket Arm' were set to music by Gillian Whitehead and performed at the Otago Festival of the Arts, 2008. Thanks to Gillian, bassoonist Ben Hoadley, pianist Emma Sayer, and to the Caselberg Trust. 'The non-singing seats' was incorporated into two etchings exhibited at Peter McLeavey Gallery, Wellington, in March 2009, with the proceeds going towards an organist's scholarship sponsored by the Maxwell Fernie Trust. Peter McLeavey read the poem at the exhibition opening, seated, with one hand upraised as if he were conducting a choir—very much in the spirit of the choirmaster Fernie. The poem was subsequently set to music by Helen Bowater and premiered at St Mary of the Angels on 25 April 2010—Maxwell Fernie's hundredth birthday. Another poem written at Peter's behest, 'Ode to Futuna Chapel', was composed for the fiftieth anniversary of the Wellington chapel on 19 March 2011.

I would like to acknowledge Bronwen Golder and the Pew Environment Group for enabling me to travel, as part of a group of artists, on HMNZS *Otago* from Auckland to Tonga, via Raoul Island, in May 2011. The poems on pages 23–31 were written during that time. It was staring into the glass eye of a nautical compass on the bridge of the *Otago* that I recognised another 'octagonal pool'—N, NE, E, SE, S, SW, W, NW—one that led off in all directions, as indeed these poems, of their own accord, seem to have done.

Some of the poems first appeared in *PNReview*, *Fulcrum*, *Heat*, *Shearsman*, *Moving Worlds*, *Metro*, the *New Zealand Listener*, *Sport*, *JAAM*, *Landfall*, the *Dominion Post*, *The Best of Best New Zealand Poems*, *The Caxton Anthology of New Zealand Poetry 1972–85* and in the on-line journals *Best New Zealand Poems*, *Jacket*, *Turbine*, *foam:e* and *Free Verse*. I am grateful to the editors of these publications. Some also appeared in the following small press editions: *Small Edible Garden* and *Finitudes* (both Fernbank Studio/Wellington Plains, 2009), *the sea of where it was we went* (Animated Figure, 2010) and *Star of Bengal Bank* (Raoul Island Publications, 2011); and in sculptor Denis O'Connor's *What the Roof Dreamt* (Aitche Books, 2007).

Many thanks to Anna Hodge, Katrina Duncan, Sam Elworthy, Christine O'Brien and Marian Hector of Auckland University Press; and to Kalee Jackson for her cover design.

And special thanks to my brother, Brendan.

Gregory O'Brien, October 2011